Save Money
Checklist Worksheet

Volume 1

Dr. Arthur H. Kebo

Save Money Checklist Worksheet – Volume 1

ISBN-13: 978-1475287561
ISBN-10: 1475287569

Book Website:

> https://www.createspace.com/3865989

WordPress Blog Website:

> http://twelvefoundations.wordpress.com/

Twitter Website:

> https://twitter.com/#!/twelvefoundatio

Facebook Website:

> http://www.facebook.com/arthurkebo

Printed in the United States of America

Table of Contents

Preface

Amidst the difficult economic times, this book was written in order to assist the individual in the financial management of daily and weekly household expenses. This workbook provides an immediately usable checklist to assist the reader in investigating his or her monthly expenses, and saving money through the use of a simple-to-use worksheet.

It is designed so that the reader can use it to identify everyday expenses, and to cut out unnecessary costs. It is often difficult to find extra income, but it is easier to eliminate wasted expenditures that one is so accustomed to in life's routine that it is quite often hidden to the average individual's awareness. It is not just a list of ideas, but a practical worksheet to plan one's weekly and monthly expenses, so that the reader can create a realistic saving's budget to work on. If an individual does not plan precisely and accurately, the determination to save money frequently becomes ambiguous and not implemented effectively, if ever implemented at all.

Just as in the construction of a building or a detailed military strategy, saving money involves actual planning by areas of cost and sub-areas, as well as determining the actual cost of each area, which allows for calculation of the exact amount that can be saved in each respective expense category. Without such a well thought out working plan, it is nearly impossible to carry out a savings plan. Vague intentions most likely will not succeed in saving you money; however, a detailed checklist serves to track your costs, making savings an actual reality. It is just like any business action plan in a commercial enterprise, which we use as executives. Unclear objectives end up not being implemented, but a detailed business plan insures real results.

It is the author's intention to provide this savings tool at minimal cost to the college student faced with rising tuition costs, the housewife dealing with rising food bills, and the average businessperson who has monthly mortgage payments and would like to save money for that vacation trip to the tropic islands with the family and never was able to, up to now.

The saving money worksheet is easy to use and does not take much time. Just grab a calculator and start going through each line of expense for every category. At the bottom of the page, you can add up the subtotal projected savings. When you add the subtotal for each category, it will give you a chance to compare your plan with the actual savings target for the week or month. The other book by the same author, *Home Economics: Budgeting & Expense Tracking Worksheet* provides you with a simple tool to calculate your budget, and worksheets to manage the day-to-day and week-to-week expenses.

Good luck on your savings plan, and that well awaited trip to the tropics!

Weekly/Monthly Projected Savings Goal Worksheet

Extra pocket money you want every week/month:

$

(Write your savings goal here.)

OR

Expense Planning Worksheet

COST FOR VACATION TRIP or WEDDING or NEW CAR or OTHER REASON FOR SAVING

DESCRIPTION	COST	QUANTITY	SUBTOTAL
	$	x	= $
	$	x	= $
	$	x	= $
	$	x	= $
	$	x	= $
	$	x	= $
	$	x	= $

TOTAL AMOUNT YOU NEED TO SAVE (By Date: / /)	$

Now, work on the worksheets for each savings category on the following pages to meet this goal, and fill in the Total Savings Calculation Worksheet at the end of this workbook to see if you have met your goal.

Savings Target Breakdown Graph

On the graph below, plot your expenses by each category percentage for last week/month to give you a general idea of your weekly/monthly expenditures. Then, plot the percentage of savings for those categories you plan to cut back for the following week/month. (Use the separate book entitled, *Home Economics: Budgeting & Expense Tracking Worksheet* by the same author, if you need to figure out your weekly/monthly expenses and manage your costs properly.)

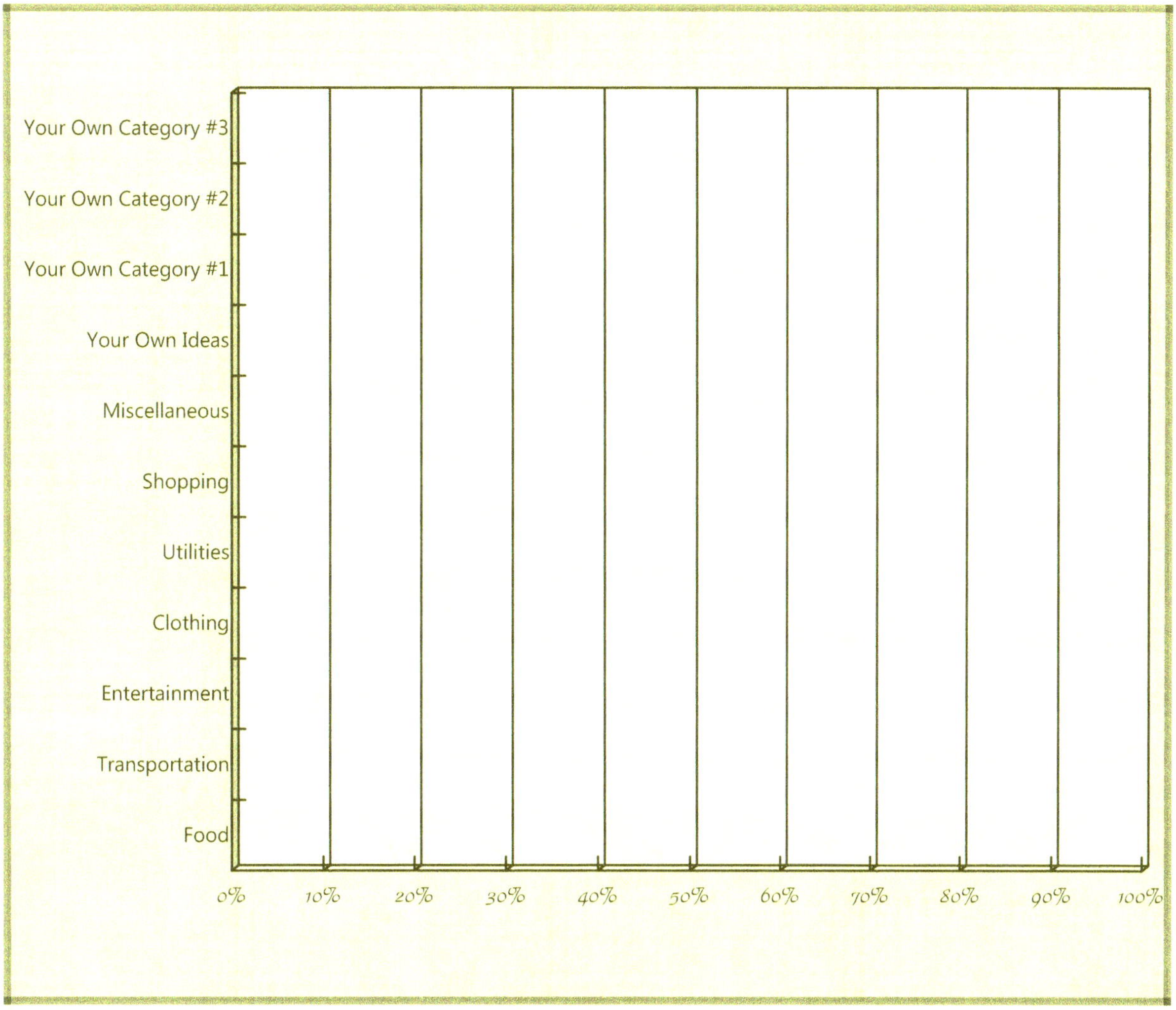

	0%	10%	20%	30%	40%	50%	60%	70%	80%	90%	100%
Your Own Category #3											
Your Own Category #2											
Your Own Category #1											
Your Own Ideas											
Miscellaneous											
Shopping											
Utilities											
Clothing											
Entertainment											
Transportation											
Food											

Now, convert those expense category percentages you plan to save next week/month into actual dollar amounts, based on your overall budget, using the worksheet on the next page.

Savings Target Calculation Worksheet

Enter the Projected Savings Goal Total from page 6 below:

PROJECTED SAVINGS GOAL TOTAL	$

Develop your Savings Target in each expense category for next week/month by converting the savings percentage for each category from page 7 to actual dollar amounts below:

EXPENSES CATEGORY	SAVINGS PERCENTAGE	AMOUNT TO SAVE
Food	%	$
Transportation	%	$
Entertainment	%	$
Clothing	%	$
Utilities	%	$
Shopping	%	$
Miscellaneous	%	$
Own Ideas	%	$
Your Own Category #1 _____	%	$
Your Own Category #2 _____	%	$
Your Own Category #3 _____	%	$

Add the subtotals on the right column to get your Savings Target Total below:

SAVINGS TARGET TOTAL	$

Now, if the Savings Target Total is greater than the Projected Savings Goal Total, enter each of these expenses category amounts on the following pages for each expenses category checklist worksheet. If the Savings Target Total is less than the Projected Savings Goal Total, go back to page 7 and figure out where else you can cut expenses, and recalculate.

Checklist Worksheet #1: Food Expenses

Enter the Savings Target for this category from page 8 below:

FOOD SAVINGS TARGET	$

1. Make your own yogurt by putting a little yogurt into a clean airtight container, pouring milk in, sealing it up in a plastic bag, and keeping it in warm water for a night.

    Amount saved on yogurt____ x $ ____ = $ ____ saved

2. Instead of going to a coffee shop, carry your own coffee in the thermos bottle.

    Number of coffee not bought ____ x $ ____ = $ ____ saved

3. Buy discounted items, priced down right before the supermarket closes, or on rainy days.

    List the amounts ____ x $ ____ = $ ____ saved
    List the amounts ____ x $ ____ = $ ____ saved
    List the amounts ____ x $ ____ = $ ____ saved

4. Check the newspaper for coupons.

    List the amounts ____ x $ ____ = $ ____ saved
    List the amounts ____ x $ ____ = $ ____ saved
    List the amounts ____ x $ ____ = $ ____ saved

5. Portion out frozen vegetables, instead of buying and wasting large amounts of fresh vegetables.

    Amount of waste saved____ x $ ____ = $ ____ saved

6. Buy extra grocery while they are on sale for expensive items, and portion them out by meal size to be stored in the freezer.

List the amounts _____ x $ _____ = $ _____ saved
List the amounts _____ x $ _____ = $ _____ saved
List the amounts _____ x $ _____ = $ _____ saved

7. Grow your own bean sprouts in a matter of days by putting cheesecloth over a bowl and rinsing the beans a couple of times a day for a few days, instead of buying expensive ones at the supermarket (i.e., lentils, chickpeas, mung beans, etc).

List the amounts _____ x $ _____ = $ _____ saved
List the amounts _____ x $ _____ = $ _____ saved
List the amounts _____ x $ _____ = $ _____ saved

8. Think of creative menus from leftover food in the refrigerator.

Amount of waste saved _____ x $ _____ = $ _____ saved

9. Buy food that does not require refrigeration, such as soup, donuts and fruits.

Estimated cost of electricity saved = $ _____ saved

10. Take a sack lunch to work, instead of dining out.

Amount saved on food cost _____ x $ _____ = $ _____ saved

11. Eat a large breakfast at home, and eat something cheaper outside for lunch with smaller amounts, such as just a salad; and take a cheap in-between snack to act as a filler-in.

Amount saved on restaurant expense _____ x $ _____ = $ _____ saved

12. From now on, eat at home before going out at night.

   Amount saved on restaurant cost and tips ____ x $ ____ = $ ____ saved

13. Search the internet for groceries that are cheaper bought in bulk amounts.

   List the amounts ____ x $ ____ = $ ____ saved
   List the amounts ____ x $ ____ = $ ____ saved
   List the amounts ____ x $ ____ = $ ____ saved

14. Carry a reusable plastic bottle around, instead of buying cans at the vending machine.

   Amount saved on drinks ____ x $ ____ = $ ____ saved

15. Cook extra portions of food, such as stew and curry and soup, apportion them by meal sizes, and store them in the freezer for another day.

   Estimated cost saved on electricity = $ ____ saved

16. Reduce consumption of excessive proteins and carbohydrates and sweets to reduce food expenses; and to prevent expensive surgeries, lab tests, hospital fees and loss of income from work days lost. (Make a daily calorie and nutrition plan!)

   Estimated food cost and medical bill saved = $ ____ saved

17. Utilize the farmer's market to buy produce directly from growers at cheaper prices.

   List the amounts ____ x $ ____ = $ ____ saved
   List the amounts ____ x $ ____ = $ ____ saved
   List the amounts ____ x $ ____ = $ ____ saved

18. Have in your mind a weekly menu based on the cheaper grocery you buy, so that you do not end up buying unnecessary items that will end up being wasted.

    Estimated cost saved on wasted food = $ _____ saved

19. Use the worksheet on the back of this workbook to record and calculate the "price per unit" of a food product, instead of always buying what seems to be the cheapest.

    List the amounts ____ x $ ____ = $ ____ saved
    List the amounts ____ x $ ____ = $ ____ saved
    List the amounts ____ x $ ____ = $ ____ saved

20. Raise a pig in your backyard, feed it food waste, use its manure for your miniature organic vegetable garden fertilizer, and eat the pig.

    Amount saved on buying ham, fertilizer and vegetables = $ ____ saved

21. _____ .

    _____ ____ x $ ____ = $ ____ saved

22. _____ .

    _____ ____ x $ ____ = $ ____ saved

23. _____ .

    _____ ____ x $ ____ = $ ____ saved

24. _____ .

    List the amounts ____ x $ ____ = $ ____ saved
    List the amounts ____ x $ ____ = $ ____ saved
    List the amounts ____ x $ ____ = $ ____ saved

25. _____ .

     List the amounts _____ x $ _____ = $ _____ saved
     List the amounts _____ x $ _____ = $ _____ saved
     List the amounts _____ x $ _____ = $ _____ saved

26. _____ .

     List the amounts _____ x $ _____ = $ _____ saved
     List the amounts _____ x $ _____ = $ _____ saved
     List the amounts _____ x $ _____ = $ _____ saved

FOOD COST SAVED SUBTOTAL	$

Checklist Worksheet #2: Transportation Expenses

Enter the Savings Target for this category from page 8 below:

TRANSPORTATION SAVINGS TARGET	$

1. Do not fill the gasoline tank to its full capacity, since the heavier the car gets, the more gasoline it will use.

   Estimated amount saved on gasoline = $ ____ saved

2. Instead of using the car wash, wipe your car on a rainy day.

   Car wash cost saved = $ ____ saved

3. Instead of wasting gasoline by getting stuck in traffic, park your car outside the city, and change to your bicycle to go into town.

   Estimated cost saved on gasoline = $ ____ saved

4. Buy something that you will need in the future, in order to get parking validation, from now on.

   Amount saved on parking ____ x $ ____ = $ ____ saved

5. Use carpool or bus instead of your car to get to work.

   Amount of money saved on gasoline ____ x $ ____ = $ ____ saved

6. Go shopping with your neighbor or friend, to save gas.

   Amount saved on gasoline ____ x $ ____ = $ ____ saved

7. Look for cheaper car insurance.

   Difference in insurance premiums = $ ____ saved

8. Research where the cheapest gas station is.

   Amount saved from difference in gas cost = $ ____ saved

9. Shop only where there is validated parking.

   Amount saved for free parking = ____ x $ ____ = $ ____ saved

10. Use the slopes to gain glide speed and prevent from pressing the breaks, as long as it is within the speed limit.

    Estimated amount saved on gasoline = $ ____ saved

11. Turn off the engine while waiting, in order to save gas.

    Estimated amount saved on gasoline = $ ____ saved

12. Buy bus or subway passes and ticket booklets, instead of buying tickets every time.

    Amount saved on tickets ____ x $ ____ = $ ____ saved

13. Use a moped for close distances, instead of a car; and save gasoline, insurance fee, repair cost, inspection fee and parking cost.

    Estimated cost saved from using moped = $ ____ saved

14. Take out unnecessary items out of the trunk that weigh the car down.

    Estimated cost of gasoline saved = $ ____ saved

15. Instead of using the heater in the car, dress warmly and use blankets.

    Estimated cost of electricity saved = $ ____ saved

16. Instead of using the air conditioner in the car, use a window sun shade.

    Estimated cost of electricity saved = $ ____ saved

17. Use the self-service pump at the gasoline station, instead of the full-service pump, from now on.

    Amount saved on gasoline service ____ x $ ____ = $ ____ saved

18. Get a car with good gas mileage or a hybrid car.

    Estimated cost saved on gasoline = $ ____ saved

19. Research the map and plan out the route so that you do not end up taking the long way or getting lost.

    Estimated cost saved on gasoline = $ ____ saved

20. Buy a huge dog, so you can put a saddle on your dog to carry the groceries back home, during its evening walk, instead of using the car for shopping.

    Amount saved on gasoline ____ x $ ____ = $ ____ saved

21. _____ .

    _____ ____ x $ ____ = $ ____ saved

22. _____ .

    _____ ____ x $ ____ = $ ____ saved

23. _____ .

   _____ ____ x $ ____ = $ ____ saved

24. _____ .

   List the amounts ____ x $ ____ = $ ____ saved
   List the amounts ____ x $ ____ = $ ____ saved
   List the amounts ____ x $ ____ = $ ____ saved

25. _____ .

   List the amounts ____ x $ ____ = $ ____ saved
   List the amounts ____ x $ ____ = $ ____ saved
   List the amounts ____ x $ ____ = $ ____ saved

26. _____ .

   List the amounts ____ x $ ____ = $ ____ saved
   List the amounts ____ x $ ____ = $ ____ saved
   List the amounts ____ x $ ____ = $ ____ saved

TRANSPORTATION COST SAVED SUBTOTAL	$

Checklist Worksheet #3: Entertainment Expenses

Enter the Savings Target for this category from page 8 below:

ENTERTAINMENT SAVINGS TARGET	$

1. Have your friends pick up the pizza or Chinese food, instead of paying delivery charges and tips.

    Amount saved on delivery charges and tips ____ x $ ____ = $ ____ saved

2. Have pot luck dinner parties, instead of dining out together.

    Amount saved on restaurants and tips $ ____ + $ ____ = $ ____ saved

3. Watch DVDs online or have them mailed to you through a special membership service with movie rental companies like Netflix.

    Amount saved on movies ____ x $ ____ = $ ____ saved

4. Go drinking only ____ days a week/month.

    Number of beers not drunk ____ x $ ____ = $ ____ saved

5. Share recorded video programs with your friends.

    Amount saved on new videos ____ x $ ____ = $ ____ saved

6. Instead of dining out for dinner, dine out for lunch, which is usually much cheaper.

    Amount saved on dining ____ x $ ____ = $ ____ saved

7. Instead of dating in places that cost money, look for free events and city-sponsored activities for entertainment.

    List the amounts _____ x $ _____ = $ _____ saved
    List the amounts _____ x $ _____ = $ _____ saved
    List the amounts _____ x $ _____ = $ _____ saved

8. Dine out at restaurants that have a discount coupon on the newspaper or website.

    Amount saved on discount _____ x $ _____ = $ _____ saved

9. Quit the fitness club and aerobic classes, and exercise in the park or get a video game fitness software or a pair of dumbbells.

    Amount saved on fitness club membership & lesson fees = $ _____ saved

10. Use the internet to search for cheap last-minute plane fare deals, when you are not in a hurry.

    Airfare saved _____ x $ _____ = $ _____ saved

11. Go on a vacation nearby, instead of a distant country.

    Amount saved on airfare or cruise ship = $ _____ saved

12. Instead of spending money to go to the movies with your friend, try varying your destination, such as a museum.

    Amount saved on movies _____ x $ _____ = $ _____ saved

13. Set up a home golf driving range or buy a video game golf and tennis software, instead of going to the golf course or tennis court for practices.

    Amount saved on golf course or tennis court cost = $ _____ saved

14. Instead of watching TV, go and exercise for free at the park.

Amount saved on electricity and cable subscription = $ ____ saved

15. Travel to cheaper locations than to expensive countries.

List the amounts ____ x $ ____ = $ ____ saved
List the amounts ____ x $ ____ = $ ____ saved
List the amounts ____ x $ ____ = $ ____ saved

16. Buy your own karaoke machine, and have concerts and song contests with your friends at home.

Amount saved on concert fees ____ x $ ____ = $ ____ saved

17. Instead of dining at the expensive hotel restaurant during your trips, stay in a room with a kitchenette or take out your meals or dine out. (The kids do not know the difference between frozen broccoli from the convenience store and a Michelin three-star restaurant *broccoli blanc de beurre*.)

Dining cost saved ____ x $ ____ = $ ____ saved

18. Instead of going out every time, stay home and build furniture or knit a sweater, and sell them at the flea market.

Amount saved on sales ____ x $ ____ = $ ____ saved

19. Instead of going around on long driving trips and picnics, buy a croquet set or volleyball net and go to the park or beach with your friends.

Estimated cost saved on gasoline = $ ____ saved

20. Instead of feeding the pigeons every time, let them feed you, by cooking the French dish, *Salmis Des Pigeons* with bacon and mushrooms.

Amount saved on pigeon feed ____ x $ ____ = $ ____ saved

21. _____ .

           _____ ____ x $ ____ = $ ____ saved

22. _____ .

           _____ ____ x $ ____ = $ ____ saved

23. _____ .

           _____ ____ x $ ____ = $ ____ saved

24. _____ .

List the amounts ____ x $ ____ = $ ____ saved
List the amounts ____ x $ ____ = $ ____ saved
List the amounts ____ x $ ____ = $ ____ saved

25. _____ .

List the amounts ____ x $ ____ = $ ____ saved
List the amounts ____ x $ ____ = $ ____ saved
List the amounts ____ x $ ____ = $ ____ saved

26. _____ .

List the amounts ____ x $ ____ = $ ____ saved
List the amounts ____ x $ ____ = $ ____ saved
List the amounts ____ x $ ____ = $ ____ saved

ENTERTAINMENT COST SAVED SUBTOTAL $

Checklist Worksheet #4: Clothing Expenses

Enter the Savings Target for this category from page 8 below:

CLOTHING SAVINGS TARGET	$

1. Wait until you have a full load for your washing machine to save water, detergent and electricity.

   Estimated cost saved on water and electricity = $ ____ saved

2. Buy clothing at the manufacturer outlet stores with minor stitch defects to save money.

   List the amounts ____ x $ ____ = $ ____ saved
   List the amounts ____ x $ ____ = $ ____ saved
   List the amounts ____ x $ ____ = $ ____ saved

3. Purchase most of your clothes during the holiday and special sales throughout the year. (Check daily newspapers for stores with current sales.) Shop around for best prices.

   List the amounts ____ x $ ____ = $ ____ saved
   List the amounts ____ x $ ____ = $ ____ saved
   List the amounts ____ x $ ____ = $ ____ saved

4. Hang your clothes outside to dry, instead of using the dryer.

   Estimated cost saved on electricity = $ ____ saved

5. Buy all your summer clothes at the end of summer, and all your winter clothes at the end of winter, in order to maximize on the clearance sales.

List the amounts _____ x $ _____ = $ _____ saved
List the amounts _____ x $ _____ = $ _____ saved
List the amounts _____ x $ _____ = $ _____ saved

6. Wash and iron simple things, instead of sending them to the cleaners. (Cleaners often fail to take out stains.)

List the amounts _____ x $ _____ = $ _____ saved
List the amounts _____ x $ _____ = $ _____ saved
List the amounts _____ x $ _____ = $ _____ saved

7. Look for cheap clothes online, instead of going to the department store.

List the amounts _____ x $ _____ = $ _____ saved
List the amounts _____ x $ _____ = $ _____ saved
List the amounts _____ x $ _____ = $ _____ saved

8. Buy regular clothes from now on, instead of brand items.

List the amounts _____ x $ _____ = $ _____ saved
List the amounts _____ x $ _____ = $ _____ saved
List the amounts _____ x $ _____ = $ _____ saved

9. If you still want brand clothes or accessories, go to the thrift shops and pawn shops in Beverley Hills, where wealthy people sell them off after wearing them only a couple of times; or where shops sell off unsold clothing.

List the amounts _____ x $ _____ = $ _____ saved
List the amounts _____ x $ _____ = $ _____ saved
List the amounts _____ x $ _____ = $ _____ saved

10. Cut back on the number of clothes you buy.

    Number of clothes you do not buy ____ x $ ____ = $ ____ saved

11. Buy fabric, and make your own clothes for clothes you wear at home.

    List the amounts ____ x $ ____ = $ ____ saved
    List the amounts ____ x $ ____ = $ ____ saved
    List the amounts ____ x $ ____ = $ ____ saved

12. Share clothes with a friend, who wears a similar size.

    List the amounts ____ x $ ____ = $ ____ saved
    List the amounts ____ x $ ____ = $ ____ saved
    List the amounts ____ x $ ____ = $ ____ saved

13. Go to clothing stores that give you points for your purchase.

    Amount saved on clothing cost = $ ____ saved

14. Experiment with scarves, reversibles, vests, belts, etc., in order to make the same clothing look completely different, instead of buying many similar clothing.

    List the amounts ____ x $ ____ = $ ____ saved
    List the amounts ____ x $ ____ = $ ____ saved
    List the amounts ____ x $ ____ = $ ____ saved

15. Stop buying clothes based on fashion trends, but buy clothes that you can continue wearing after the trend ends.

    List the amounts ____ x $ ____ = $ ____ saved
    List the amounts ____ x $ ____ = $ ____ saved
    List the amounts ____ x $ ____ = $ ____ saved

16. Instead of buying new clothes every time you lose weight or gain weight, just tailor your clothes to refit your size.

List the amounts _____ x $ _____ = $ _____ saved
List the amounts _____ x $ _____ = $ _____ saved
List the amounts _____ x $ _____ = $ _____ saved

17. Check with friends who had babies to see if they have old baby clothes that can be shared.

Amount saved on baby clothes _____ x $ _____ = $ _____ saved

18. Get stretchable clothes if you are pregnant or a middle-aged man with a pot belly, instead of buying larger clothes every time.

List the amounts _____ x $ _____ = $ _____ saved
List the amounts _____ x $ _____ = $ _____ saved
List the amounts _____ x $ _____ = $ _____ saved

19. Move to a warmer climate, so you do not have to buy winter clothes.

List the amounts _____ x $ _____ = $ _____ saved
List the amounts _____ x $ _____ = $ _____ saved
List the amounts _____ x $ _____ = $ _____ saved

20. Have your all your babies in rapid succession, since handed-down baby clothes to younger siblings will go out of fashion very fast.

List the amounts _____ x $ _____ = $ _____ saved
List the amounts _____ x $ _____ = $ _____ saved
List the amounts _____ x $ _____ = $ _____ saved

21. _____ .

_____ _____ x $ _____ = $ _____ saved

22. _____ .

 _____ ____ x $ ____ = $ ____ saved

23. _____ .

 _____ ____ x $ ____ = $ ____ saved

24. _____ .

List the amounts ____ x $ ____ = $ ____ saved
List the amounts ____ x $ ____ = $ ____ saved
List the amounts ____ x $ ____ = $ ____ saved

25. _____ .

List the amounts ____ x $ ____ = $ ____ saved
List the amounts ____ x $ ____ = $ ____ saved
List the amounts ____ x $ ____ = $ ____ saved

26. _____ .

List the amounts ____ x $ ____ = $ ____ saved
List the amounts ____ x $ ____ = $ ____ saved
List the amounts ____ x $ ____ = $ ____ saved

CLOTHING COST SAVED SUBTOTAL	$

Checklist Worksheet #5: Utilities Expenses

Enter the Savings Target for this category from page 8 below:

UTILITIES SAVINGS TARGET	$

1. Put plastic bubble wraps on the bedroom windows during the winter for insulation.

   Estimated cost of electricity saved = $ ____ saved

2. Cancel channels not watched on cable TV or cancel entire cable TV.

   Cost of cable TV saved = $ ____ saved

3. Cancel telephone land line, and use only cell phone.

   Cost of telephone land line saved = $ ____ saved

4. Wear warm clothes or cool clothes, and limit heater or cooler use.

   Estimated cost decreased for heater and cooler = $ ____ saved

5. Turn on the fan for a few seconds to circulate the warm air from the heater, which tends to accumulate by the ceiling, since warm air rises and cold air sinks to the floor.

   Approximate cost decreased for heater and cooler = $ ____ saved

6. Unplug appliances when not in use, or use an extension cord with on/off switches.

   Estimated cost of electricity saved from unnecessary drain = $ ____ saved

7. Calculate whether it is cheaper to pay the electricity bill by check, automatic monthly bank withdrawal or credit card.

   Amount saved = $ ____ saved

8. Turn off lights in rooms which you are not using.

   Estimated cost of electricity saved = $ ____ saved

9. Move any furniture beforehand, so that you do not waste electricity by moving furniture during the vacuuming.

   Estimated cost of electricity saved = $ ____ saved

10. Use the microwave to cook vegetables, make soup and heat water.

    Estimated cost of electricity and water saved = $ ____ saved

11. Avoid using the telephone. Instead, use the e-mail, post cards and fax.

    Estimated cost of telephone saved = $ ____ saved

12. Pay your bills online, instead of spending postage costs.

    Amount saved on postage costs = $ ____ saved

13. Drop unnecessary telephone special services.

    Cost of telephone special services saved = $ ____ saved

14. Do not keep the water running. Fill the basin or cup with water, when brushing your teeth or washing your face.

    Estimated cost of water saved = $ ____ saved

15. Find a cheaper internet provider and free internet phone.

Difference in cost = $ ____ saved

16. Turn the shower off while soaping up the body. Use the shower only for rinsing.

Estimated cost of water saved = $ ____ saved

17. Cool the food before placing it in the refrigerator.

Estimated cost of electricity saved = $ ____ saved

18. Stay by the window where the sunshine is, during the cold winter, and close the curtains, during the hot summer to conserve heater/cooler costs. Use the sunlight to work, instead of the room's light, whenever possible.

Estimated cost of electricity saved = $ ____ saved

19. Unplug the air conditioner during the winter season to save electricity drain.

Estimated cost of electricity saved = $ ____ saved

20. Put a timer on your teenage daughter's phone, or make her pay a percentage of her telephone bill from her allowance.

Estimated amount saved on telephone bill = $ ____ saved

21. _____ .

   _____ ____ x $ ____ = $ ____ saved

22. _____ .

   _____ ____ x $ ____ = $ ____ saved

23. _____ .

   _____ ____ x $ ____ = $ ____ saved

24. _____ .

   List the amounts ____ x $ ____ = $ ____ saved
   List the amounts ____ x $ ____ = $ ____ saved
   List the amounts ____ x $ ____ = $ ____ saved

25. _____ .

   List the amounts ____ x $ ____ = $ ____ saved
   List the amounts ____ x $ ____ = $ ____ saved
   List the amounts ____ x $ ____ = $ ____ saved

26. _____ .

   List the amounts ____ x $ ____ = $ ____ saved
   List the amounts ____ x $ ____ = $ ____ saved
   List the amounts ____ x $ ____ = $ ____ saved

UTILITIES COST SAVED SUBTOTAL	$

Checklist Worksheet #6: Shopping Expenses

Enter the Savings Target for this category from page 8 below:

SHOPPING SAVINGS TARGET	$

1. Instead of buying something while in the store or after watching the TV commercial, wait a few days to think it over to decide if you really need it or if it will end up rusting in your closet (need versus want).

   List the amounts _____ x $ _____ = $ _____ saved
   List the amounts _____ x $ _____ = $ _____ saved
   List the amounts _____ x $ _____ = $ _____ saved

2. Write down the store name and price that had the cheapest price for a product, so that you remember where the most inexpensive store is, and you buy all the cheapest items at each store. (Use the worksheet at the end of this workbook.)

   List the amounts _____ x $ _____ = $ _____ saved
   List the amounts _____ x $ _____ = $ _____ saved
   List the amounts _____ x $ _____ = $ _____ saved

3. Buy last year's model of the electrical appliances, right after the new one comes out.

   List the amounts _____ x $ _____ = $ _____ saved
   List the amounts _____ x $ _____ = $ _____ saved
   List the amounts _____ x $ _____ = $ _____ saved

4. Research on the net before purchasing merchandise for durability statistics and point services and price differences.

    Estimated amount saved on repair, points and price $ ____ saved

5. Buy energy-saver type electrical appliances.

    Estimated cost saved every week/month = $ ____ saved

6. Buy used items at the recycle shops, instead of brand new items.

    List the amounts ____ x $ ____ = $ ____ saved
    List the amounts ____ x $ ____ = $ ____ saved
    List the amounts ____ x $ ____ = $ ____ saved

7. Buy computers and clothes that are on display for cheaper discounted prices, after checking for good condition.

    Amount saved off normal price ____ x $ ____ = $ ____ saved

8. Check the internet auction for large purchases.

    Amount saved by buying through auction = $ ____ saved

9. Ask for generic brand drugs and generic merchandise instead of brand name items.

    List the amounts ____ x $ ____ = $ ____ saved
    List the amounts ____ x $ ____ = $ ____ saved
    List the amounts ____ x $ ____ = $ ____ saved

10. Use the DVD/CD plastic containers to wind extra cables in them.

    Amount saved on cable storage cases = $ ____ saved

11. Buy books and merchandise and clothes on the same website to save delivery cost and gain points.

Approximate amount saved on delivery cost and points = $ ____ saved

12. Check for store closeout sales or new opening store sales to take advantage of them.

List the amounts ____ x $ ____ = $ ____ saved
List the amounts ____ x $ ____ = $ ____ saved
List the amounts ____ x $ ____ = $ ____ saved

13. Feed the kids before going shopping, or else, they will want to eat outside.

Amount saved on meals outside ____ x $ ____ = $ ____ saved

14. Search for small specialized stores around your neighborhood that may be cheaper than the larger supermarkets and department stores.

Estimated cost saved on lower prices = $ ____ saved

15. Use the old plastic CD cases to file your store coupons in, and place them in alphabetical order in a box.

Amount saved on file folders ____ x $ ____ = $ ____ saved

16. Search the internet for office supplies and household goods that are cheaper bought in bulk amounts.

List the amounts ____ x $ ____ = $ ____ saved
List the amounts ____ x $ ____ = $ ____ saved
List the amounts ____ x $ ____ = $ ____ saved

17. Use yogurt containers to sort out and organize your desk, as well as your kitchen and garage cabinets.

Amount saved on office, kitchen and garage supplies = $ ____ saved

18. Make a monthly budget sheet, to prevent overspending.

Estimated cost saved from overspending = $ ____ saved

19. E-mail digital Christmas cards with animation, instead of buying cards and using postage stamps.

Amount saved on Christmas cards and postage stamps = $ ____ saved

20. Use sterilized leaves from the backyard, instead of buying toilet paper.

Amount saved on toilet paper ____ x $ ____ = $ ____ saved

21. _____ .

_____ ____ x $ ____ = $ ____ saved

22. _____ .

_____ ____ x $ ____ = $ ____ saved

23. _____ .

_____ ____ x $ ____ = $ ____ saved

24. _____ .

List the amounts ____ x $ ____ = $ ____ saved
List the amounts ____ x $ ____ = $ ____ saved
List the amounts ____ x $ ____ = $ ____ saved

25. _____ .

     List the amounts _____ x $ _____ = $ _____ saved
     List the amounts _____ x $ _____ = $ _____ saved
     List the amounts _____ x $ _____ = $ _____ saved

26. _____ .

     List the amounts _____ x $ _____ = $ _____ saved
     List the amounts _____ x $ _____ = $ _____ saved
     List the amounts _____ x $ _____ = $ _____ saved

SHOPPING COST SAVED SUBTOTAL	$

Checklist Worksheet #7: Miscellaneous Expenses

Enter the Savings Target for this category from page 8 below:

MISCELLANEOUS SAVINGS TARGET	$

1. Use internet banks that provide cheaper service due to no labor cost.

    Amount saved on cheaper fees ____ x $ ____ = $ ____ saved

2. Have a garage sale every few months to get rid of unwanted items around the house.

    List the amounts ____ x $ ____ = $ ____ saved
    List the amounts ____ x $ ____ = $ ____ saved
    List the amounts ____ x $ ____ = $ ____ saved

3. When mailing documents or items, use the flat rate envelopes and boxes from the post office.

    List the amounts ____ x $ ____ = $ ____ saved
    List the amounts ____ x $ ____ = $ ____ saved
    List the amounts ____ x $ ____ = $ ____ saved

4. Sell your house, and buy a cheaper one.

    Amount saved on mortgage payments ____ x $ ____ = $ ____ saved

5. Cut back on subscriptions to magazines.

    Amount saved on magazine subscriptions ____ x $ ____ = $ ____ saved

6. Get a bank debit card, instead of a credit card.

    Amount saved on credit card fees and interests = $ ____ saved

7. Negotiate apartment leases so that there is no overlap in rent with the previous place.

    Amount saved on apartment rent = $ ____ saved

8. Move to a state that has lower taxes, and cost of living is less.

    Estimated cost saved on taxes and living costs = $ ____ saved

9. Buy a fix-it-yourself book, instead of hiring a carpenter or plumber or roof tile layer or gardener or mason.

    Amount saved on expensive home repairs ____ x $ ____ = $ ____ saved

10.   With the money you save from using this checklist worksheet plan, use it to pay off extra premium on your mortgage, in order to lower the monthly payments on your house.

    Amount saved on monthly mortgage payments = $ ____ saved

11.   Put an ad out for roommates who you can rent out your extra bedrooms to.

    Amount saved on additional income from rent = $ ____ saved

12.   Change to a free checking account which has no fees, and move whatever extra money you have to a savings account that yields higher interest.

    Amount saved on fees and additional interests = $ ____ saved

13. Get a copy of the workbook entitled, "Home Economics: Budgeting & Expense Tracking" by the same author, in order to manage your finances better by budgeting every week/month and tracking your expenses.

    Amount saved on unnecessary costs and proper planning = $ ____ saved

14. Itemize your deductions on college expenses that are tax-deductible.

    Amount saved on taxes = $ ____ saved

15. Make your own pet food out of food waste.

    Amount saved on pet food ____ x $ ____ = $ ____ saved

16. Check what kind of employee benefits you have, and maximize on those.

    Amount saved on employee benefits ____ x $ ____ = $ ____ saved

17. Arrange with a friend to share newspaper subscriptions: they can read it in the morning, and you can read at lunch time.

    Amount saved on newspaper subscriptions ____ x $ ____ = $ ____ saved

18. Do a simple hairstyle yourself, instead of going to the beauty parlor every time.

    Amount saved on beauty parlor cost ____ x $ ____ = $ ____ saved

19. Stop buying lottery tickets or going to horse races, which have very little possibility of return; but rather, invest in something that has greater interest or dividend.

    Cost saved on lottery tickets and horse races ____ x $ ____ = $ ____ saved

20. Praise your husband on how magnificent a gardener he is and how no one can do a better job than he can, instead of having him lie around watching TV and hiring a contract gardener.

Amount saved on gardening fees _____ x $ _____ = $ _____ saved

21. _____

_____ _____ x $ _____ = $ _____ saved

22. _____ .

_____ _____ x $ _____ = $ _____ saved

23. _____ .

_____ _____ x $ _____ = $ _____ saved

24. _____ .

List the amounts _____ x $ _____ = $ _____ saved
List the amounts _____ x $ _____ = $ _____ saved
List the amounts _____ x $ _____ = $ _____ saved

25. _____ .

List the amounts _____ x $ _____ = $ _____ saved
List the amounts _____ x $ _____ = $ _____ saved
List the amounts _____ x $ _____ = $ _____ saved

26. _____ .

    List the amounts ____ x $ ____ = $ ____ saved
    List the amounts ____ x $ ____ = $ ____ saved
    List the amounts ____ x $ ____ = $ ____ saved

MISCELLANEOUS COST SAVED SUBTOTAL	$

Checklist Worksheet #8: Your Own Ideas For Expense Savings

Enter the Savings Target for this category from page 8 below:

YOUR OWN IDEAS SAVINGS TARGET	$

1. _____ .

   _____ ____ x $ ____ = $ ___ saved

2. _____ .

   _____ ____ x $ ____ = $ ___ saved

3. _____ .

   _____ ____ x $ ____ = $ ___ saved

4. _____ .

   _____ ____ x $ ____ = $ ___ saved

5. _____ .

   _____ ____ x $ ____ = $ ___ saved

6. _____ .

   _____ ____ x $ ____ = $ ___ saved

7. _____ .

   _____ ____ x $ ____ = $ ___ saved

8. _____ .

   _____ ____ x $ ____ = $ ____ saved

9. _____ .

   _____ ____ x $ ____ = $ ____ saved

10. _____ .

    _____ ____ x $ ____ = $ ____ saved

11. _____ .

    List the amounts ____ x $ ____ = $ ____ saved
    List the amounts ____ x $ ____ = $ ____ saved
    List the amounts ____ x $ ____ = $ ____ saved

12. _____ .

    List the amounts ____ x $ ____ = $ ____ saved
    List the amounts ____ x $ ____ = $ ____ saved
    List the amounts ____ x $ ____ = $ ____ saved

13. _____ .

    List the amounts ____ x $ ____ = $ ____ saved
    List the amounts ____ x $ ____ = $ ____ saved
    List the amounts ____ x $ ____ = $ ____ saved

14. _____ .

    List the amounts ____ x $ ____ = $ ____ saved
    List the amounts ____ x $ ____ = $ ____ saved
    List the amounts ____ x $ ____ = $ ____ saved

15. _____ .

    List the amounts _____ x $ _____ = $ _____ saved
    List the amounts _____ x $ _____ = $ _____ saved
    List the amounts _____ x $ _____ = $ _____ saved

16. _____ .

    List the amounts _____ x $ _____ = $ _____ saved
    List the amounts _____ x $ _____ = $ _____ saved
    List the amounts _____ x $ _____ = $ _____ saved

17. _____ .

    List the amounts _____ x $ _____ = $ _____ saved
    List the amounts _____ x $ _____ = $ _____ saved
    List the amounts _____ x $ _____ = $ _____ saved

18. _____ .

    List the amounts _____ x $ _____ = $ _____ saved
    List the amounts _____ x $ _____ = $ _____ saved
    List the amounts _____ x $ _____ = $ _____ saved

19. _____ .

    List the amounts _____ x $ _____ = $ _____ saved
    List the amounts _____ x $ _____ = $ _____ saved
    List the amounts _____ x $ _____ = $ _____ saved

20. _____ .

      List the amounts ____ x $ ____ = $ ____ saved
      List the amounts ____ x $ ____ = $ ____ saved
      List the amounts ____ x $ ____ = $ ____ saved

COST SAVED FOR YOUR OWN IDEAS SUBTOTAL	$

Checklist Worksheet #9: Your Own Category #1 Savings

Enter the Savings Target for this category from page 8 below:

YOUR OWN CATEGORY #1 SAVINGS TARGET _____	$

1. _____ .

    _____ ____ x $ ___ = $ ___ saved

2. _____ .

    _____ ____ x $ ___ = $ ___ saved

3. _____ .

    _____ ____ x $ ___ = $ ___ saved

4. _____ .

    _____ ____ x $ ___ = $ ___ saved

5. _____ .

    _____ ____ x $ ___ = $ ___ saved

6. _____ .

    _____ ____ x $ ___ = $ ___ saved

7. _____ .

    _____ ____ x $ ___ = $ ___ saved

8. _____ .

    _____ ____ x $ ____ = $ ____ saved

9. _____ .

    _____ ____ x $ ____ = $ ____ saved

10. _____ .

    _____ ____ x $ ____ = $ ____ saved

11. _____ .

    List the amounts ____ x $ ____ = $ ____ saved
    List the amounts ____ x $ ____ = $ ____ saved
    List the amounts ____ x $ ____ = $ ____ saved

12. _____ .

    List the amounts ____ x $ ____ = $ ____ saved
    List the amounts ____ x $ ____ = $ ____ saved
    List the amounts ____ x $ ____ = $ ____ saved

13. _____ .

    List the amounts ____ x $ ____ = $ ____ saved
    List the amounts ____ x $ ____ = $ ____ saved
    List the amounts ____ x $ ____ = $ ____ saved

14. _____ .

    List the amounts ____ x $ ____ = $ ____ saved
    List the amounts ____ x $ ____ = $ ____ saved
    List the amounts ____ x $ ____ = $ ____ saved

15. _____ .

    List the amounts _____ x $ _____ = $ _____ saved
    List the amounts _____ x $ _____ = $ _____ saved
    List the amounts _____ x $ _____ = $ _____ saved

16. _____ .

    List the amounts _____ x $ _____ = $ _____ saved
    List the amounts _____ x $ _____ = $ _____ saved
    List the amounts _____ x $ _____ = $ _____ saved

17. _____ .

    List the amounts _____ x $ _____ = $ _____ saved
    List the amounts _____ x $ _____ = $ _____ saved
    List the amounts _____ x $ _____ = $ _____ saved

18. _____ .

    List the amounts _____ x $ _____ = $ _____ saved
    List the amounts _____ x $ _____ = $ _____ saved
    List the amounts _____ x $ _____ = $ _____ saved

19. _____ .

    List the amounts _____ x $ _____ = $ _____ saved
    List the amounts _____ x $ _____ = $ _____ saved
    List the amounts _____ x $ _____ = $ _____ saved

20. _____ .

      List the amounts ____ x $ ____ = $ ____ saved
      List the amounts ____ x $ ____ = $ ____ saved
      List the amounts ____ x $ ____ = $ ____ saved

COST SAVED FOR YOUR OWN CATEGORY #1 SUBTOTAL	$

Checklist Worksheet #10: Your Own Category #2 Savings

Enter the Savings Target for this category from page 8 below:

| YOUR OWN CATEGORY #2 SAVINGS TARGET _____ | $ |

1. _____ .

   _____ ____ x $ ____ = $ ____ saved

2. _____ .

   _____ ____ x $ ____ = $ ____ saved

3. _____ .

   _____ ____ x $ ____ = $ ____ saved

4. _____ .

   _____ ____ x $ ____ = $ ____ saved

5. _____ .

   _____ ____ x $ ____ = $ ____ saved

6. _____ .

   _____ ____ x $ ____ = $ ____ saved

7. _____ .

   _____ ____ x $ ____ = $ ____ saved

8. _____ .

    _____ ____ x $ ____ = $ ____ saved

9. _____ .

    _____ ____ x $ ____ = $ ____ saved

10. _____ .

    _____ ____ x $ ____ = $ ____ saved

11. _____ .

    List the amounts ____ x $ ____ = $ ____ saved
    List the amounts ____ x $ ____ = $ ____ saved
    List the amounts ____ x $ ____ = $ ____ saved

12. _____ .

    List the amounts ____ x $ ____ = $ ____ saved
    List the amounts ____ x $ ____ = $ ____ saved
    List the amounts ____ x $ ____ = $ ____ saved

13. _____ .

    List the amounts ____ x $ ____ = $ ____ saved
    List the amounts ____ x $ ____ = $ ____ saved
    List the amounts ____ x $ ____ = $ ____ saved

14. _____ .

    List the amounts ____ x $ ____ = $ ____ saved
    List the amounts ____ x $ ____ = $ ____ saved
    List the amounts ____ x $ ____ = $ ____ saved

15. _____ .

    List the amounts _____ x $ _____ = $ _____ saved
    List the amounts _____ x $ _____ = $ _____ saved
    List the amounts _____ x $ _____ = $ _____ saved

16. _____ .

    List the amounts _____ x $ _____ = $ _____ saved
    List the amounts _____ x $ _____ = $ _____ saved
    List the amounts _____ x $ _____ = $ _____ saved

17. _____ .

    List the amounts _____ x $ _____ = $ _____ saved
    List the amounts _____ x $ _____ = $ _____ saved
    List the amounts _____ x $ _____ = $ _____ saved

18. _____ .

    List the amounts _____ x $ _____ = $ _____ saved
    List the amounts _____ x $ _____ = $ _____ saved
    List the amounts _____ x $ _____ = $ _____ saved

19. _____ .

    List the amounts _____ x $ _____ = $ _____ saved
    List the amounts _____ x $ _____ = $ _____ saved
    List the amounts _____ x $ _____ = $ _____ saved

20. _____ .

List the amounts ____ x $ ____ = $ ____ saved

List the amounts ____ x $ ____ = $ ____ saved

List the amounts ____ x $ ____ = $ ____ saved

COST SAVED FOR YOUR OWN CATEGORY #2 SUBTOTAL	$

Checklist Worksheet #11: Your Own Category #3 Savings

Enter the Savings Target for this category from page 8 below:

YOUR OWN CATEGORY #3 SAVINGS TARGET	_____	$

1. _____ .

   _____ ____ x $ ____ = $ ____ saved

2. _____ .

   _____ ____ x $ ____ = $ ____ saved

3. _____ .

   _____ ____ x $ ____ = $ ____ saved

4. _____ .

   _____ ____ x $ ____ = $ ____ saved

5. _____ .

   _____ ____ x $ ____ = $ ____ saved

6. _____ .

   _____ ____ x $ ____ = $ ____ saved

7. _____ .

   _____ ____ x $ ____ = $ ____ saved

8. _____ .

    _____ ____ x $ ____ = $ ____ saved

9. _____ .

    _____ ____ x $ ____ = $ ____ saved

10. _____ .

    _____ ____ x $ ____ = $ ____ saved

11. _____ .

    List the amounts ____ x $ ____ = $ ____ saved
    List the amounts ____ x $ ____ = $ ____ saved
    List the amounts ____ x $ ____ = $ ____ saved

12. _____ .

    List the amounts ____ x $ ____ = $ ____ saved
    List the amounts ____ x $ ____ = $ ____ saved
    List the amounts ____ x $ ____ = $ ____ saved

13. _____ .

    List the amounts ____ x $ ____ = $ ____ saved
    List the amounts ____ x $ ____ = $ ____ saved
    List the amounts ____ x $ ____ = $ ____ saved

14. _____ .

    List the amounts ____ x $ ____ = $ ____ saved
    List the amounts ____ x $ ____ = $ ____ saved
    List the amounts ____ x $ ____ = $ ____ saved

15. _____ .

    List the amounts ____ x $ ____ = $ ____ saved
    List the amounts ____ x $ ____ = $ ____ saved
    List the amounts ____ x $ ____ = $ ____ saved

16. _____ .

    List the amounts ____ x $ ____ = $ ____ saved
    List the amounts ____ x $ ____ = $ ____ saved
    List the amounts ____ x $ ____ = $ ____ saved

17. _____ .

    List the amounts ____ x $ ____ = $ ____ saved
    List the amounts ____ x $ ____ = $ ____ saved
    List the amounts ____ x $ ____ = $ ____ saved

18. _____ .

    List the amounts ____ x $ ____ = $ ____ saved
    List the amounts ____ x $ ____ = $ ____ saved
    List the amounts ____ x $ ____ = $ ____ saved

19. _____ .

    List the amounts ____ x $ ____ = $ ____ saved
    List the amounts ____ x $ ____ = $ ____ saved
    List the amounts ____ x $ ____ = $ ____ saved

20. _____ .

      List the amounts ___ x $ ___ = $ ___ saved

      List the amounts ___ x $ ___ = $ ___ saved

      List the amounts ___ x $ ___ = $ ___ saved

COST SAVED FOR YOUR OWN CATEGORY #3 SUBTOTAL	$

Savings Calculation Worksheet

Enter the Savings Subtotals for each category from the other pages below:

SAVINGS DESCRIPTION	SUBTOTAL
Food Cost Saved	+$
Transportation Cost Saved	+$
Entertainment Cost Saved	+$
Clothing Cost Saved	+$
Utilities Cost Saved	+$
Shopping Cost Saved	+$
Miscellaneous Cost Saved	+$
Cost Saved For Your Own Ideas	+$
Cost Saved For Your Own Category #1 _____	+$
Cost Saved For Your Own Category #2 _____	+$
Cost Saved For Your Own Category #3 _____	+$

Add the Savings Subtotals on the right column and enter the Savings Total below:

SAVINGS TOTAL	=$

Enter the Savings Target Total from page 8 below:

SAVINGS TARGET TOTAL	−$

Subtract the Savings Target Total from the Savings Total to arrive at your Total Balance:

TOTAL BALANCE	=$

If your Total Balance is a positive number, you have met your Savings Target. If your Total Balance is a negative number, you need to go back to each worksheet and find out where you can cut additional expenses. If you need to manage and track your expenditures every week/month, use the separate book entitled, *Home Economics: Budgeting & Expense Tracking Worksheet* by the same author.

Discount Coupon Filing Record Sheet
(by alphabetical listing)

PRODUCT NAME STARTING WITH:				A
COUPON #	PRODUCT	STORE	EXPIRATION DATE	NOTES

PRODUCT NAME STARTING WITH:				B
COUPON #	PRODUCT	STORE	EXPIRATION DATE	NOTES

PRODUCT NAME STARTING WITH:				C
COUPON #	PRODUCT	STORE	EXPIRATION DATE	NOTES

PRODUCT NAME STARTING WITH:				D
COUPON #	PRODUCT	STORE	EXPIRATION DATE	NOTES

PRODUCT NAME STARTING WITH:				E
COUPON #	PRODUCT	STORE	EXPIRATION DATE	NOTES

PRODUCT NAME STARTING WITH:				F
COUPON #	PRODUCT	STORE	EXPIRATION DATE	NOTES

PRODUCT NAME STARTING WITH:				G
COUPON #	PRODUCT	STORE	EXPIRATION DATE	NOTES

PRODUCT NAME STARTING WITH:				H
COUPON #	PRODUCT	STORE	EXPIRATION DATE	NOTES

PRODUCT NAME STARTING WITH:			I	
COUPON #	PRODUCT	STORE	EXPIRATION DATE	NOTES

PRODUCT NAME STARTING WITH:			J	
COUPON #	PRODUCT	STORE	EXPIRATION DATE	NOTES

PRODUCT NAME STARTING WITH:				K
COUPON #	PRODUCT	STORE	EXPIRATION DATE	NOTES

PRODUCT NAME STARTING WITH:				L
COUPON #	PRODUCT	STORE	EXPIRATION DATE	NOTES

PRODUCT NAME STARTING WITH:				M
COUPON #	PRODUCT	STORE	EXPIRATION DATE	NOTES

PRODUCT NAME STARTING WITH:				N
COUPON #	PRODUCT	STORE	EXPIRATION DATE	NOTES

PRODUCT NAME STARTING WITH:				O
COUPON #	PRODUCT	STORE	EXPIRATION DATE	NOTES

PRODUCT NAME STARTING WITH:				P
COUPON #	PRODUCT	STORE	EXPIRATION DATE	NOTES

PRODUCT NAME STARTING WITH:				Q & R
COUPON #	PRODUCT	STORE	EXPIRATION DATE	NOTES

PRODUCT NAME STARTING WITH:				S
COUPON #	PRODUCT	STORE	EXPIRATION DATE	NOTES

PRODUCT NAME STARTING WITH:				T
COUPON #	PRODUCT	STORE	EXPIRATION DATE	NOTES

PRODUCT NAME STARTING WITH:				U & V
COUPON #	PRODUCT	STORE	EXPIRATION DATE	NOTES

PRODUCT NAME STARTING WITH:				W
COUPON #	PRODUCT	STORE	EXPIRATION DATE	NOTES

PRODUCT NAME STARTING WITH:				X & Y & Z
COUPON #	PRODUCT	STORE	EXPIRATION DATE	NOTES

Cheapest Store Record Sheet
(for regularly bought items)

STORE NAME:		ADDRESS:		

DATE	PRODUCT	PRICE	AT NUMBER OF ITEMS	NOTES
/ /		$	@	
/ /		$	@	
/ /		$	@	
/ /		$	@	
/ /		$	@	
/ /		$	@	
/ /		$	@	
/ /		$	@	

STORE NAME:		ADDRESS:		

DATE	PRODUCT	PRICE	AT NUMBER OF ITEMS	NOTES
/ /		$	@	
/ /		$	@	
/ /		$	@	
/ /		$	@	
/ /		$	@	
/ /		$	@	
/ /		$	@	
/ /		$	@	

| STORE NAME: | | ADDRESS: | | |

DATE	PRODUCT	PRICE	AT NUMBER OF ITEMS	NOTES
/ /		$	@	
/ /		$	@	
/ /		$	@	
/ /		$	@	
/ /		$	@	

| STORE NAME: | | ADDRESS: | | |

DATE	PRODUCT	PRICE	AT NUMBER OF ITEMS	NOTES
/ /		$	@	
/ /		$	@	
/ /		$	@	
/ /		$	@	
/ /		$	@	

| STORE NAME: | | ADDRESS: | | |

DATE	PRODUCT	PRICE	AT NUMBER OF ITEMS	NOTES
/ /		$	@	
/ /		$	@	
/ /		$	@	
/ /		$	@	
/ /		$	@	

STORE NAME:		ADDRESS:		

DATE	PRODUCT	PRICE	AT NUMBER OF ITEMS	NOTES
/ /		$	@	
/ /		$	@	
/ /		$	@	
/ /		$	@	
/ /		$	@	

STORE NAME:		ADDRESS:		

DATE	PRODUCT	PRICE	AT NUMBER OF ITEMS	NOTES
/ /		$	@	
/ /		$	@	
/ /		$	@	
/ /		$	@	
/ /		$	@	

STORE NAME:		ADDRESS:		

DATE	PRODUCT	PRICE	AT NUMBER OF ITEMS	NOTES
/ /		$	@	
/ /		$	@	
/ /		$	@	
/ /		$	@	
/ /		$	@	

STORE NAME: **ADDRESS:**

DATE	PRODUCT	PRICE	AT NUMBER OF ITEMS	NOTES
/ /		$	@	
/ /		$	@	
/ /		$	@	
/ /		$	@	
/ /		$	@	
/ /		$	@	
/ /		$	@	
/ /		$	@	
/ /		$	@	
/ /		$	@	
/ /		$	@	

STORE NAME: **ADDRESS:**

DATE	PRODUCT	PRICE	AT NUMBER OF ITEMS	NOTES
/ /		$	@	
/ /		$	@	
/ /		$	@	
/ /		$	@	
/ /		$	@	
/ /		$	@	
/ /		$	@	
/ /		$	@	
/ /		$	@	
/ /		$	@	
/ /		$	@	

STORE NAME:		ADDRESS:		

DATE	PRODUCT	PRICE	AT NUMBER OF ITEMS	NOTES
/ /		$	@	
/ /		$	@	
/ /		$	@	
/ /		$	@	
/ /		$	@	
/ /		$	@	
/ /		$	@	
/ /		$	@	
/ /		$	@	
/ /		$	@	
/ /		$	@	

STORE NAME:		ADDRESS:		

DATE	PRODUCT	PRICE	AT NUMBER OF ITEMS	NOTES
/ /		$	@	
/ /		$	@	
/ /		$	@	
/ /		$	@	
/ /		$	@	
/ /		$	@	
/ /		$	@	
/ /		$	@	
/ /		$	@	
/ /		$	@	
/ /		$	@	

STORE NAME: **ADDRESS:**

DATE	PRODUCT	PRICE	AT NUMBER OF ITEMS	NOTES
/ /		$	@	
/ /		$	@	
/ /		$	@	
/ /		$	@	
/ /		$	@	
/ /		$	@	
/ /		$	@	
/ /		$	@	
/ /		$	@	
/ /		$	@	
/ /		$	@	

STORE NAME: **ADDRESS:**

DATE	PRODUCT	PRICE	AT NUMBER OF ITEMS	NOTES
/ /		$	@	
/ /		$	@	
/ /		$	@	
/ /		$	@	
/ /		$	@	
/ /		$	@	
/ /		$	@	
/ /		$	@	
/ /		$	@	
/ /		$	@	
/ /		$	@	

Words Of Advice

Congratulations! You have finished planning for your savings, and are now on that road to making that extra money every week or every month.

It just takes thinking each item through carefully; getting the plan on paper; and diligently adhering to that plan—this means no candy bar at the convenience store on your walk back with your dog which adds that extra inch on your waist , or keeping that television on while you are not watching it.

It is important that you keep the receipt for each expense, record them, and track your costs carefully to meet each category target in your action plan. You can get the separate workbook entitled, *Home Economics: Budgeting & Expense Tracking Worksheet* by the same author, which will help you calculate your weekly/monthly budget and track your expenses accurately, in order to manage your finances.

Every success starts with a plan; and every plan starts with keeping it. Good luck!

Helpful References

Fix-It-Yourself Handbooks

1) New Fix-It-Yourself Manual: How to Repair, Clean, and Maintain Anything and Everything In and Around Your Home (by Reader's Digest)
   Publisher: Reader's Digest
   ISBN: 978-0895778710

2) Black & Decker The Complete Photo Guide to Home Repair: with 350 Projects and 2000 Photos (by Editors of Creative Publishing)
   Publisher: Creative Publishing International
   ISBN: 978-1589234178

3) Floors, Stairs & Carpets (by Time-Life Books)
   Publisher: Sunset Publishing Company
   ISBN: 978-0376019097

Cheap Travel Comparison Guides

1) The World's Cheapest Destinations: 21 Countries Where Your Money is Worth a Fortune (by Tim Leffel)
   Publisher: Booklocker.com, Inc.
   ISBN: 978-1601457011

2) The Encyclopedia of Cheap Travel: Save Up to 90% on Fights, Lodging, Cruises, and More! (by Terrance Zepke)
   Publisher: Lookout Publishing
   ISBN: 978-0615514727

3) How To Travel the World When You Can't Afford it: The Secret of my Travel Success (by Laurie Goldsmith)
   Publisher: CreateSpace
   ISBN: 978-1470097424

Cooking Cheap Meals Books

1) The $5 a Meal College Cookbook: Good Cheap Food for When You Need to Eat (by Rhonda Lauret Parkinson and B.E. Horton)
   Publisher: Adams Media
   ISBN: 978-1440502088

2) Healthy Meals for Less: Great-Tasting Simple Recipes Under $1 a Serving (by Jonni McCoy)
   Publisher: Bethany House Publishers
   ISBN: 978-0764207105

3) Better Homes and Gardens Budget-Friendly Meals (by Better Homes & Gardens)
   Publisher: Wiley
   ISBN: 978-0470540282

Growing Your Own Balcony Garden Materials

1) Vertical Vegetables & Fruits: Creative Gardening Techniques for Growing Up in Small Spaces (by Rhonda Massingham Hart)
   Publisher: Storey Publishing, LLC
   ISBN: 978-1603429986

2) Starter Vegetable Gardens: 24 No-Fail Plans for Small Organic Gardens (by Barbara Pleasant)
   Publisher: Storey Publishing, LLC
   ISBN: 978-1603425292

3) The Vegetable Gardener's Container Bible: How to Grow a Bounty of Food in Pots, Tubs, and Other Containers (by Edward C. Smith)
   Publisher: Storey Publishing, LLC
   ISBN: 978-1603429757

Recycle Used Clothes Books

1) New From Old: How to Transform and Customize Your Clothes (by Jayne Emerson)
   Publisher: Firefly Books
   ISBN: 1554072042

2) How to Recycle old clothes into new fashions (by Fenya Crown)
   Publisher: Prentice-Hall
   ISBN: 978-0134308197

3) Born-Again Vintage: 25 Ways to Deconstruct, Reinvent, and Recycle Your Wardrobe (by Bridgett Artise and Jen Karetnick)
   Publisher: Potter Craft
   ISBN: 978-0307405272

Other Resources Available

Home Economics: Budgeting & Expense Tracking Worksheet

by Dr. Arthur H. Kebo

at

https://www.createspace.com/3865989

Save Money Checklist Worksheet – Volume 2

by Dr. Arthur H. Kebo

at

https://www.createspace.com/3865993